# FLORIDA

# FLORIDA
## Valerie Bodden

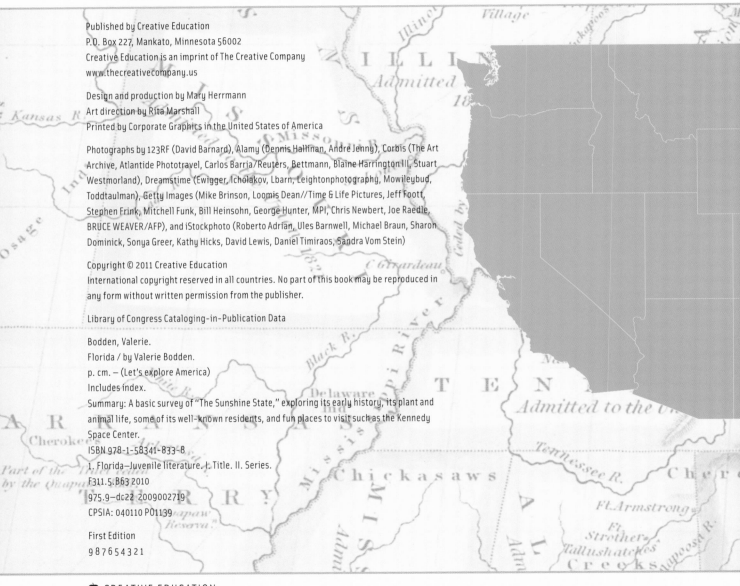

Published by Creative Education
P.O. Box 227, Mankato, Minnesota 56002
Creative Education is an imprint of The Creative Company
www.thecreativecompany.us

Design and production by Mary Herrmann
Art direction by Rita Marshall
Printed by Corporate Graphics in the United States of America

Photographs by 123RF (David Barnard), Alamy (Dennis Hallinan, Andre Jenny), Corbis (The Art Archive, Atlantide Phototravel, Carlos Barria/Reuters, Bettmann, Blaine Harrington III, Stuart Westmorland), Dreamstime (Ewigger, Icholakov, Lbarn, Leightonphotography, Mowileybud, Toddtaulman), Getty Images (Mike Brinson, Loomis Dean//Time & Life Pictures, Jeff Foott, Stephen Frink, Mitchell Funk, Bill Heinsohn, George Hunter, MPI, Chris Newbert, Joe Raedle, BRUCE WEAVER/AFP), and iStockphoto (Roberto Adrian, Ules Barnwell, Michael Braun, Sharon Dominick, Sonya Greer, Kathy Hicks, David Lewis, Daniel Timiraos, Sandra Vom Stein)

Library of Congress Cataloging-in-Publication Data

Bodden, Valerie.
Florida / by Valerie Bodden.
p. cm. — (Let's explore America)
Includes index.
Summary: A basic survey of "The Sunshine State," exploring its early history, its plant and animal life, some of its well-known residents, and fun places to visit such as the Kennedy Space Center.
ISBN 978-1-58341-833-8
1. Florida—Juvenile literature. I. Title. II. Series.
F311.5.B63 2010
975.9—dc22 2009002719
CPSIA: 040110 PO1139

First Edition
9 8 7 6 5 4 3 2 1

 CREATIVE EDUCATION

TOP, THEN LEFT TO RIGHT:
- *A golf course next to a Florida beach*
- *An old map showing Florida*
- *A surfer*
- *An iguana, a lizard common to Florida*
- *Sailboats on a Florida beach*

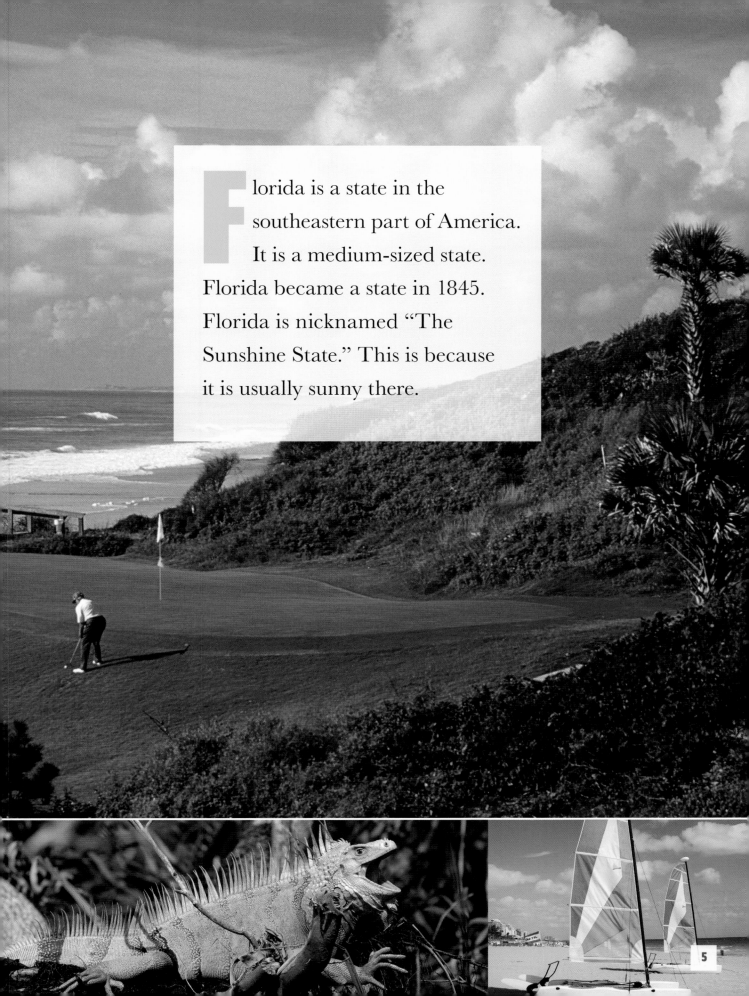

Florida is a state in the southeastern part of America. It is a medium-sized state. Florida became a state in 1845. Florida is nicknamed "The Sunshine State." This is because it is usually sunny there.

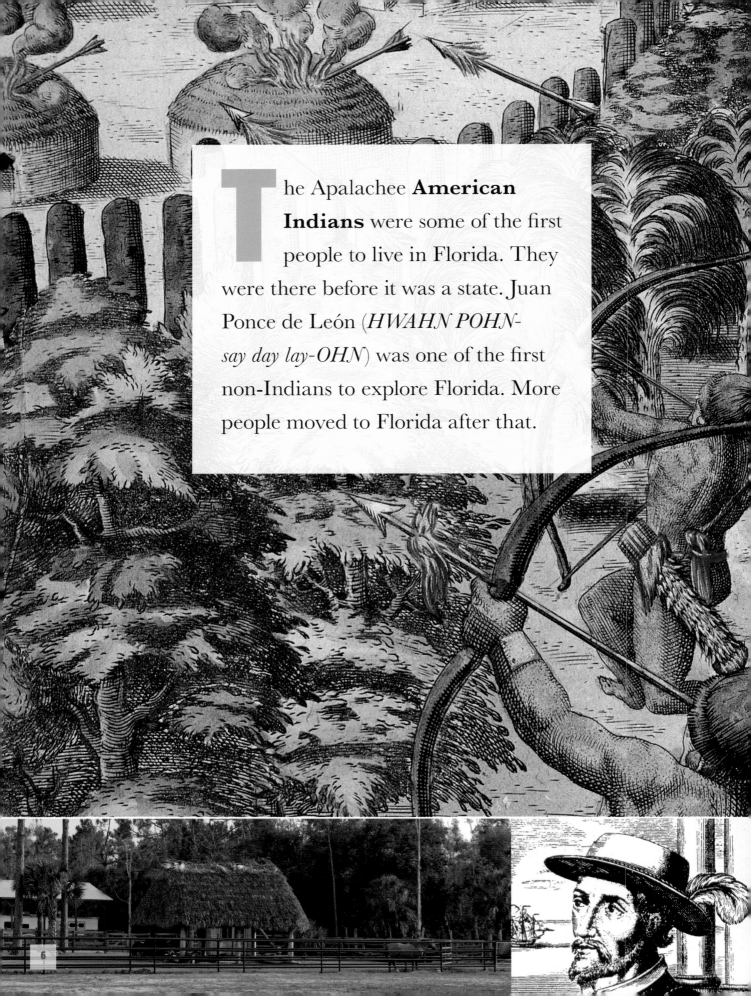

The Apalachee **American Indians** were some of the first people to live in Florida. They were there before it was a state. Juan Ponce de León (*HWAHN POHN-say day lay-OHN*) was one of the first non-Indians to explore Florida. More people moved to Florida after that.

TOP, THEN LEFT TO RIGHT:

- American Indians in Florida
- The farm of an Indian family in Florida
- Explorer Juan Ponce de León
- A Florida Indian leader named Osceola
- People from other countries getting ready to move to Florida

TOP, THEN LEFT TO RIGHT:

- *The Everglades wetland*
- *A surfer on a Florida beach*
- *A boy flying a kite*
- *A big sea animal called a manatee*

**F**lorida is next to the Atlantic Ocean and the Gulf of Mexico. It has lots of beaches. There is a big **wetland** called the Everglades in southern Florida. Florida's weather is usually warm.

armers in Florida grow oranges, strawberries, and corn. Mangrove, beech, and palm trees grow in Florida. Deer and black bears live in the state. So do alligators.

TOP, THEN LEFT TO RIGHT:
- An alligator
- Mangrove trees in a wetland
- An ear of corn
- Palm trees
- A Florida deer

Florida's state flower is the orange blossom. The orange blossom is a white flower that grows on orange trees. Florida's state bird is the mockingbird. The mockingbird is a small, white and gray bird. Florida's state tree is the sabal (*SAY-bal*) palm. The sabal palm has long leaves.

TOP, THEN LEFT TO RIGHT:
- *Orange trees*
- *An orange blossom*
- *A sabal palm tree*
- *A mockingbird*

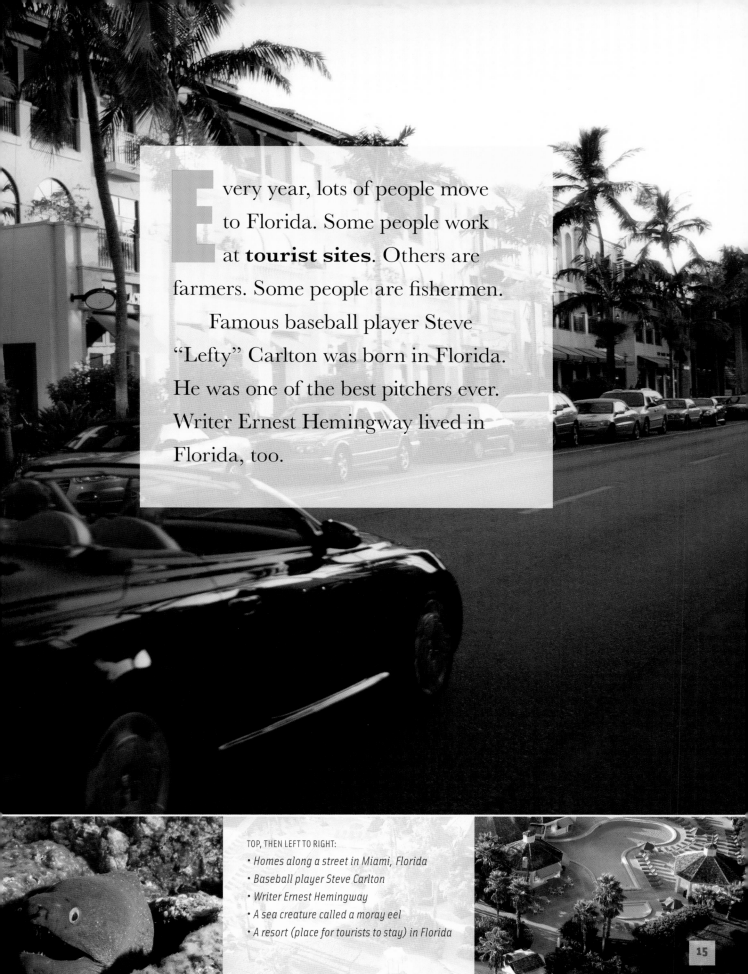

Every year, lots of people move to Florida. Some people work at **tourist sites**. Others are farmers. Some people are fishermen.

Famous baseball player Steve "Lefty" Carlton was born in Florida. He was one of the best pitchers ever. Writer Ernest Hemingway lived in Florida, too.

TOP, THEN LEFT TO RIGHT:
• *Homes along a street in Miami, Florida*
• *Baseball player Steve Carlton*
• *Writer Ernest Hemingway*
• *A sea creature called a moray eel*
• *A resort (place for tourists to stay) in Florida*

15

Jacksonville is the biggest city in Florida. Almost 800,000 people live there. Tallahassee is the capital of Florida. The capital is where people in the **government** make decisions about laws for the state.

TOP, THEN LEFT TO RIGHT:
- A bridge and buildings in Jacksonville, Florida
- A shopping center in Jacksonville
- The state capitol (main government building) in Tallahassee
- Statues of children playing in Tallahassee
- The Florida Supreme Court building in Tallahassee

Every year, lots of people go to Walt Disney World amusement park in Florida. Others go to the Kennedy Space Center to see space shuttles. Some people go **scuba diving**. Florida offers lots of fun in the sun!

TOP, THEN LEFT TO RIGHT:
- *Cinderella Castle at Walt Disney World*
- *Fish in the ocean near Florida*
- *The colorful lights of Miami*
- *A girl playing at the beach*

## FACTS ABOUT FLORIDA

**First year as a state:** *1845*

**Population:** *18,537,969*

**Capital:** *Tallahassee*

**Biggest city:** *Jacksonville*

**Nickname:** *The Sunshine State*

**State bird:** *mockingbird*

**State flower:** *orange blossom*

**State tree:** *sabal palm*

*People parasailing
(flying through the air using
a rope and parachute)*

Long bridges that connect
Florida islands

## GLOSSARY

**American Indians**—people who lived in America before white people arrived

**government**—a group that makes laws for the people of a state or country

**scuba diving**—swimming underwater using an air tank to breathe

**tourist sites**—places that lots of travelers visit

**wetland**—an area where the land is very wet all of the time

## READ MORE

Bredeson, Carmen. *Florida*. New York: Children's Press, 2002.

Crane, Carol. *S Is for Sunshine: A Florida Alphabet*. Chelsea, Mich.: Sleeping Bear Press, 2000.

## LEARN MORE

Enchanted Learning: Florida
http://www.enchantedlearning.com/usa/states/florida/index.shtml
This site has Florida facts, maps, and coloring pages.

Kids Konnect: Florida
http://www.kidskonnect.com/content/view/173/27
This site lists facts about Florida.

A space shuttle at the
Kennedy Space Center